Invisible Orchestras

Joy Gaines-Friedler
and
Ron Riekki

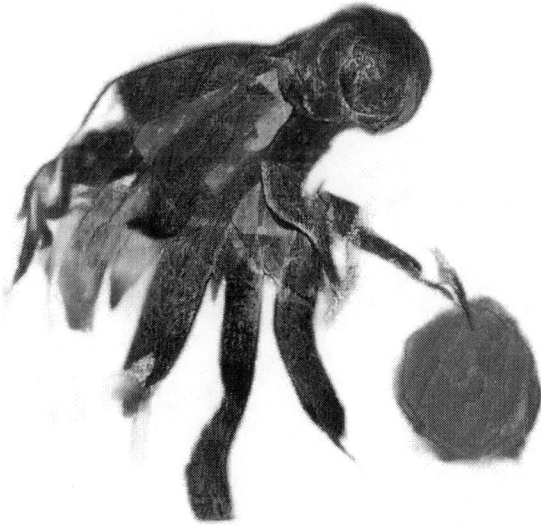

Cholla Needles Arts & Literary Library
Joshua Tree, CA

front cover/title page art by Tsui Ling Toomer
back cover art by Hoàng Thi LÊ

https://www.chollaneedles.com
a non-profit corporation

ISBN: 9798396634510

There are nights when the wolfs are silent,
and only the moon howls.
-George Carlin

to Eric Torgersen
for teaching brevity

Invisible Orchestras

Widow

      for Joanne

I've learned to put salt in the softener, to pay
the bills with no reluctance. I've learned
to fill the empty sections on the calendar.
I can phone a roofer should I need to,
take the car in for alignment. Every day I wake
to the same light through our bedroom window
to the same absence, to the same alarm.

I love

the orchestra
of night,
how the moon
sounds
like cellos
if you listen
with your soul.

Getting Rid of the Spider

He said, I can't cure her
missing childhood. Can't be
her hero, replace her un-mothering.
I can only crack open this beer,
listen to the crickets,
hope their calls don't sound
too much like loneliness to her.

On the night she broke up with me

I went   to put out   the garbage

and looked up   in time   to see

the Space   Shuttle   taking off.

It looked like an airplane   on fire.

I kind   of wished   it was.

Fireflies

At times we synchronize our flashing,
sew light, like surgeon's thread, into the heart

wound. It was once like that, a surgeon told me, before
they could temporarily stop the heart

they would thread in rhythm to its pulse;
thread, pump, thread, pump, thread.

Delicate is love. Delicate, it requires a steady beat,
a small pulsating light. Body seeking body.

Seven, I Knew Lightning

wouldn't strike me so I'd go outside in the rain and look up, straight at the grey, the howl, the bats of rain, the bad shoulder of my dad in the window, and I'd dare God to do it, but he never would. He'd just throw water in my face. And I'd drink it. God, we did that a lot of nights, me and God. We were idiots.

How We Love Our Parents

We leave a list of disasters by the telephone
in case they call:

The sump-pump broke
The basement flooded.

The garage floor is cracked.
Our circular saw was stolen.

They respond with lots of oh-nos
and oh for God's sake.

It is how we make them happy.

On Not Getting Hired

It's OK. I have knees. My hotel
is in my back. I think I've tried to commit

suicide so many times that the election year
doesn't even complain anymore.

Remember Julie? God, she was perfect.
Now there's just Mom's ashes. It gets worse.

Listen to this. I'm barefeet in a Publix
and the woman owner is telling me to leave,

so I go home, get on match.com and the first
woman I click on looks so sad that I wonder

if she just got stabbed by a Chinese grad student.
Remember Julie? God, she was beautiful.

When I think about taking pills, it's like a light
breeze. I don't even have to take them.

Christ, I remember what it was like
to have a job. It was like crashing.

Children's Hospital

I am nine & in the admissions waiting room.

A girl the color of sunset watches me
pull a puzzle from a box under the bench.

Maybe she knows I've done this before.
Maybe she knows I come here often.

Maybe she knows I am ashamed of that.
Her name is called. Our eyes meet.

For an instant we are sisters with a secret
neither of us will ever speak of.

Love Poem, Cincinnati

I wanted to marry my girlfriend
so I pretended she was pregnant,
convincing her we had to marry,
        that the baby was coming,
that it was just outside the window,
                just outside the door,
        that it was coming up the steps,
                almost in our bedroom
                        and she said to stop,
                        that I was making the baby
sound like a serial killer, that she'd seen movies like that,
with the knife coming closer and closer and closer until she
held her hand inches from my nose, an invisible knife gripped,
ready, to kill the first baby in sight.

Dear Euphrosyne (U-froze-a-nay)
Goddess of Good Cheer

Come on. I know you are out there. I've felt your presence early in life – you know, those times you saved me. I remember how you claimed the dark hallways of the hospital, showed me how to be the one to make a game out of those old geezer wheelchairs. Us kids that could get out of bed did some racing with those old things. And, when I felt lonely there you showed up on the face of an orderly offering me cookies and apple juice. And, now? I need you more than ever. The world is a tsunami, it's a wildfire. Thanks for sending me that silly turkey hen, the tom, and their 8 poults. Stanley Kunitz says we have to learn to live with our own frailties. Dear, dear Euphrosyne, I apologize for the bunson burner I keep in my back pocket.

Dr. James Crow

He sits us all down, piled on the bench, says

even if you love the unemployment,

even if you love the drugs, you have to turn

to the walls of health care, theirs, get caught up

in the courts; it's part of the slave-anthem,

the echoes of the future. Here is you—hopeful.

Here is you—fucked. The sky all filled

with God. Of course, it's not your sky.

Yours is filled with smoke. They call it

clouds. Don't let them fool you.

Another Field

Yes, I too
want

another field
on a summer

day – a blanket
our skin

water

the motion
and rhythm

of bees

Poem about a Werewolf That I Copied from Shakespeare

The moon—that's where it starts. Of course,
you can't begin with birth, something so obvious,
the claws coming out breech, or going back
even earlier, the lycanthropic spermatozoa.
Goddamnit, I'm never going to be able to get
to Finland now, not on scholarship anyway.
To do that, you need to write poems about history
or paintings or, if you're really good at branding
yourself, the history of painting. People eat that
shit up. Actually, they don't. We pretend they do.

Touch

A chickadee lands in your hand.
Its body a buoy.

It grips your finger.
You don't hold it. It holds you.

It is a kiss, both hard & soft,
both lip & bone.

On your way about your life,
at the mailbox or a stop light,

your body remembers
those feathers. That touch. & others.

My Upper Peninsula

I've read a few poems entitled "My Upper Peninsula."
They were all written by people who don't live there.

The poems seemed to lack suffering or fire, the flames
that sawed the world in half when I was eight, trees

left as slash marks across the land, a home caught up
in the triggers of the world, the way that poems

mislead, can give voice to visitors, can burn down
everything you ever knew with one tourist's match.

Escape From Crete

Icarus
my love
how you cherished
your life. How you
flew through it creating stars
inside people who loved you dearest.
Your animal wings were the feathered hands
that stroked the sky. They were the strong
touch of spine on skin. You left me in
this labyrinth of illusion. Left me with only the sun.

Ron Riekki

The Sun, It Occasionally Sets in Grand Marais, Michigan
"The strongest castle, tower, and town,
The golden bullet beats it down."
--Shakespeare, "The Passionate Pilgrim"

Grand Marais, you are not a town.
You are a horseshoe. You are thrown
over and over and over again against metal,
pounding your head against the disowned.
Grand Marais, you are no town.
You're a small nightmare of scratch marks on the back
of a masturbator, a campground with a broken
generator, your Christmases stamped to the ground.
Grand Marais, I'm sorry, but I'm going to have to say
fuck you. I don't mean that I want to have sex
with your church steeples or your insane water tower
hovering above the world like a big fat crucifix.
 I mean, that I want you to give me back
 the cousin that you drowned.

19

Daffodils

The street we walked home from school was austere, trees twiggy saplings of suburbia; houses compact repetitions of life after war; the neighborhood a slender girl with an expense account, a purse to match each outfit. No lush gardens, just a few spring flowers outside Mrs. Goddeson's house. What did I know of bulbs, or the hands that planted them? I left the sidewalk even though it meant non-conformity, crossed her carpet of lawn then pulled on the thick stems that would not release. Someone was sure to see me. Someone was already marking me. I pulled at the stubborn flowers until I felt something tear. A breaking from its roots. A release. Frightened and willing I held the whole of it. I was responsible for this life – this beautiful death.

My Girlfriend Loves to Point Out My Mistakes

It's exhaustive, thunderclap repetitions
of forks in wrong places. I don't make the bed
the right way. I didn't know there was a right way.
I thought there was just a bed, a driveway, a car, a home.

She says I don't fall down the stairs correctly. She tumbles,
her necking snapping, the legs like two enemies of the ground,
the shriveling at the bottom of the stairs.

There's something so impressively Evil Dead about it.
I say she's right.
I tell her to step aside.
 I throw myself down

three flights. She tells me to forget it.
She'll throw everything down the steps herself.
I watch the bed go, the plants, the lamp, the neighbors,
the funeral, the priest, the talk,
 God.
They all fall with such precision.

Too Much Yes

Where is that part of *no*
that forms at the mouth
so sure of itself

it can beat up the boys?

Laid down like a word,
a broken tree limb,
like a blackout.

Something lives at the end of *no*.
Something, not like a flower,
but rather, like the moon.

Solid. Concrete. Immovable.

Rudolf Otto

At a fair in Lille, I think of Das Heilige.
Something about the spinning of children,
their screams of ecstasy, triggers the awe

of Otto, the way he saw God in all of these
numinous moments, the sky so large we
feel as if we're being swallowed, the odd

love of the stars, where the ghosts of sky
wink; in the middle of a thousand people,
I look straight up, waiting to be salvaged.

Time

I steal the marrow of memory, leave you
only the bone, but don't worry
I will take that too.

Your loves still walk with you
in measurable periods – small
movements, first touches, cigarettes

lifted to lips, hands on steering wheels.
You've got your photographs

but what you don't know, what you can't
know is how much has changed

& how much further there is to go.

Clive Staples Lewis

I wish I could surprise the world
with joy, lead you from closets
to snow; I think how the word

lion means hero, how he'd set
up characters who all would
change so significantly, sunsets

of souls, their lives whirled
to whole new rich mindsets,
learning from what they wished.

Florida Traffic Poem

Indifference is a form of bullying
as is crowding you out, and diverting
attention – the way my brother
would place his small fingers
on my grandfather's chin to pull him
away from me. Hands I later became afraid of;
the coda of fists between the lanes of my shoulders.
I was forced to wait a long time for the damn lights
to change. But isn't that the thing about traffic lights?
The pattern goes on and on and on. The cars change
but the pattern does not. You get in your car,
you better expect it.

The Guy Sitting in the Park Alone, Snow Falling

I'm sure he's never murdered anyone.
He has a book in his pocket and that's a good sign.
The snow is falling on him, so he's not a ghost.
He looks cold, so he's human.
Maybe I'm the one to worry about,
staring at him through a window,
standing in my underwear,
a Detroit Lions lamp nearby,
which is the worst team in the history of organized sports.
And this guy as lonely as a chandelier in a mansion,
the boring white sky ceilings of the rich.

The Garage

I wanted to be invented.
I wanted to be cleaned & polished,
lifted, torqued, calibrated.
I wanted to be as immaculate as your power tools.
Air compressed. I wanted you to be my Craftsman
Chest. Casted smooth, your vacuum, chrome plated,
mirrored. I wanted to be hand polished, scanned,
hooked-up to your diagnostics. I wanted Bose speakers
installed in me. I wanted combustion. But here is where
you said you show me what you can do for me.
And what you cannot.

I Hate the Famous

I'd set their fuel-drums on fire,
brick their foreheads
if I could only wrap up their rich

indoor sun and break it
into eighty wardrobes.
There are those who stumble

into shut up. They have their job
to do, and by to do, I mean
to have sex with, to impregnate

work—of course, it's really the work
of others, of Others, of the great
orgasm of the dying poor.

I'm Tired of Loss

of losing at Dodgeball, losing my favorite uncle
to suicide, who hasn't lost a dog or cat or goldfish?
And what of the losing seasons? Our team lost – boo fucking hoo.
I lost three pregnancies – the last on the floor in my bedroom – loss
of future – no guarantees. Despite my learning to bolt, dodge,
dance around his anger, my father used to say,
You'll miss me when I'm gone. Loss: the story of The Fall.
And Jim from HIV. And Linda from those bullets,
the loss of sanity, loss of treatment for her husband's loss of mind.
Let's fill our prisons with losses. Who isn't lost? The lost shirt I loved
(to love a shirt is itself a loss). Loss of feeling in my baby finger
from the trimmer blade. Oh loss, what you do is grim.
I really miss my dad.

Sonnet 6: I'm a Dork
for Tara

I'm a sugarplum fairy, a blueberry cock, the cop
who lets you off, a sugarcane cunt. I'm a belly-
flop, a Corina Copp, a missing mistress with
a corridor toy. I'm a dark-chocolate martyr,
a metal-head EMT b-boy. I'm a levitating failure,
a cougar, a sorghum banshee. I pop mo'er-
fucks. I shop in the shittiest malls. I cough
so much that my cologne's Halls. I stop traffic
for nothing, throwing rocks on medians. I'm smelly—
brain full of spies, garlic in my asshole. I'm a cork,
a forty-foot pole. I'm a poet, which means I'm Spock
without the intelligence. I'm a Dirk Diggler
without the abundance. A pre-steroid Carrot Top.
A Tarot deck warning sign. A goblin with a Valentine.

Miscarriage

Last night the barn across the street
burst into flames.

First sound that rumbled like a moan.
Then terror.

The fire screamed the way a scream
remains silent through other screams.

There was no stopping this.
Time traveled back toward birth –

a revelation of its dubious skeleton
infused with the smell of budding bones.

Suddenly lifeless – an empty space.
The morning drifted in ash.

Ron Riekki

When He Goes Out to Spit
for Bonnie Jo Campbell

I live with the Buddhists
in a dorm
and am getting used to
the cursing.
It's strange, hearing
the f-word
from a monk,
but we all have
language and rage
and the huge Buddha
on the wall
sits there
with me
staring at His mouth.

Her Medicine

Today I inched my way toward the sound
of a woman's confession
at the checkout counter
… my beautiful daughter…
as if reaching toward bus diesel streets,
cast iron grates, broken fragments
of glass, … *committed suicide.*

Confession at the checkout counter
in a store that sells Hallmark cards
and creamy ceramic baskets filled
with plastic pastel eggs, Anita Baker
singing *You Bring Me Joy.* I inched
my way closer, wanting to hear
more about the kids who couldn't
find their mother. Her voice a plea,
then silent as the float of space
after a siren. Someone asked what
happened.

We gathered around her, offering
sacred herb and sweet grass, hoping
to be her medicine. We circled her.
Strangers in a Hallmark store
handing her what we could.

Rat-a-tat
for Lisa Fay Coutley

As the poem goes, so does the poet.
I'm not black. I'm not white. I'm Greek.
I keep wondering if I'm Jewish.
Here is a throat. Here is a bone.
Even the gods can be killed
in ways that would make medics cringe.
I'm sorry you think I'm crazy.
I was just trying hard to make poetry
be heard. It's hard, this desk,
this night, this time. I'm thinking
of becoming a pair of ballet slippers.
I feel, then, that maybe I could slip
into a suicide note and end it with
something hopeful where the child
would live, would lick the wind,
the wick, the lack of everything, gone.

Like Vapor

My mother is the cloud's
misty edges
soon she will disappear.
Again

I draw her with color pencil;
white pencil on white
paper;
gray on gray.

She is the fog that hovers
above the quiet water
dissolved by sunlight
at dawn.

A Cousin Got to be a Zombie on The Walking Dead

It will be the high point of his life.
Although he gets higher than the tractors
on the farm down the street.

He looks all silver now,
basking in the heat of success,
if you can call a left-hook

a right-hook. I remember
when we'd look at the Sears
catalogue lingerie. It was like

finding out your dog didn't die.
It was like finding out Christmas
was tomorrow, again, so you can drag

the burned tree back into the house
for more presents to ensure poverty.
But it was better than that, the loss of eyes.

A Bedouin Girl On a Hill in Israel

Wearing a blood red quabbeh around her chest
and hips. Red against the skeleton of a rusted

pickup truck. Red against tank beige
sand and Mediterranean blue. An Acheulian

Goddess she stands in sandals
on a hill overlooking the busy highway.

She is holding a dead cat by its hind legs.

She holds it away from her as though its oily stench
will taint her; as though she's done this before.

Her arm is not tired.

From the highway I see her walk to the edge.
I watch her let it let go.

Writing This on the Divinity School Lawn

The sky keeps trying to get thinner.
I say that it needs to gain weight.
We want a sky with its stomach full.

Who wants a sky too slim to hold stars?
We should all breathe as much air as possible.
Do it now. Hold it in your family of lungs.

I want to get in there, hug you like an alligator,
tell you that you are even more beautiful
than the bottle of rum above my fridge.

A Mother Story

1.
Begins with hands—long,
nails polished night smooth.
You run your fingertips over their firm surety.
Woman sequined, all curve and body.
Woman as Redbud, wide, full of flower.

2.
She is a tree beside a grove of trees.
When the sky closes around her
she becomes solemn, blameful—as if a deer
has snapped a branch from her.

3.
A birthday party. the knotty pine basement.
A blue circus cake. Pin-The-Tail-On-The-Donkey.
Disoriented by the spin. No one finds the proper spot.
No one can. She never notices
the donkey taped too high.

I Had a Librarian Tell Me That Poetry Chapbooks are Only Good for Firewood

When I taught in prison, I told the prisoners
that if they murder someone on the page,
they can win an award, but if you murder

someone in real life, you'll end up back
here in prison. One of the guys raised

his hand and said, What if you kill the person

who gives you the award? The class liked that.

Joy Gaines-Friedler

Counting Change

Nine at night. My mother sits on the edge

of her bed. The window a dark painting, still

outside I see the white-robed shadow of a heron.

As the sun rose this morning

my father died. Now, my mother sits on the edge

of their bed. She has emptied the contents

of a blue jar calculating what's left.

I am standing in the doorway watching. I know

that whatever my father left won't be enough.

Mom, I say, *Do you believe in heaven?*

Not really, she answers without a penny's

worth of hesitation, without ever looking up.

Ron Riekki

Life Goes So Fast That It Scares the Hell Out of Me

It leaves a purgatory in my gut.
There's a heaven somewhere in there too,
thirsty.

On The News Hour Fifteen More Names

as they become available. I call a friend
to bridge some distance, maybe

get some reassurance. She talks wine & vodka.
I call another. Her voice bells a declaration:

her "path is a spiritual journey," she tries only
"to live in a place of love." I want them to know

that my lost ones follow me. They follow
me to the grocery store, to the river.

In hallways they chatter among themselves.
Even my unborns who have grown up.

Meanwhile, the names stream by in silence.
There are no names for the survivors.

Ron Riekki

This Poem is about a Small Town in the Upper Peninsula of Michigan and a College I Hated in Massachusetts

I lit a basketball on fire and rolled it into the gym.
In divinity school, they sure the hell talked about sex
a lot. They'd see penises in their coffee. I wanted to punch
half the class in the face. It reminded me of high
school when all the pot-heads used to stand on the corner

and smoke cigarettes. All the jocks would be on the bus
not playing any sports. Nobody ever does want they want.
We all end up with feet like pancakes. Our necks turn
into failed cyborg parts that no longer turn. I wish
I'd have lit the gym on fire and saved the basketball.

Flies

They fly toward the light always
toward the light which makes it easy

to lure them to where I can electrocute
them with a battery operated swatter,

or where the cat, despite her arthritic joints,
her failing back legs, grabs focus,

sets her sites. It's their wings,
the way they flutter—& desire

fills her. Primal & distinct
she becomes exactly

what she needs them to make of her;
a killer, a monster.

My savior.

Confessions X

I worked in a prison psych ward.
How the hell do I explain that to you?
It was in Florida.
There were guys in there who would rip their stomachs open.
You could see their colons.
You could see their intestines.
They'd look at me and smile, Can I go to the hospital?

I used to walk ten miles to Marquette as a kid.
Then I'd walk ten miles back.
There wasn't anything else to do.

On the way to a baseball game, a group of kids beat me until my shoulder blade was disconnected. They stopped when they saw that.

I remember walking away and one of the kids followed me, staring at me like I was an art piece, as if he had made something beautiful. He said something to me and I just said, yeah, yeah, yeah, yeah, and I kept walking in the direction where I thought the clinic was. I could tell my shoulder was at a forty-five degree angle.

I looked like a monster.
The blood was everywhere.
The glove was in my good hand.
I remember walking and I felt empty and proud.
This is true—I actually remember thinking,
You're not going to kill me, no one can ever kill me
and the sun was like a railroad on fire.

Sonnet

Something in you wants to love this life.
Wants it Polynesian, full of sea spark,
hard bodied, and in the evenings, profiles
of trees, a hammock against some
ridiculously perfect sky. Something wants
the juice of peaches to sweeten your tongue, wants
the hum of flame, crackle of wood spark.
Something in you wants to be speared,
honey spread, be an orange pillowed chair,
a blue vase, forsythia blooming on old wood.
But, then there's that toaster oven and dishwasher.
Their mock finish gone pitted with rust
from your damp rag. Really, all you wanted was
to shine things up a bit, wipe them clean.

Matcha

We sit in a teashop, looking down
at three fish. They are good
at communicating how hungry they are.

The tea isn't very good.
It's expensive.

There are over 3.6 million prisoners
in the U.S. and China.

Battles

Large woman up against small—I'm used to that
said, *you don't know* – you don't "no" nothin'- when you should.

Hands on her wide hips she
glared at me, *my people, my people...*

but, I told her, *my people too*
and the others. I crossed an icy bridge

between buildings and wound up with a theatre group.
I listened as a beautiful woman, hair white as wolf's teeth,
said, I'm a thespian – I'm proud.

The large woman caught up to me
know, nobody going to care unless you do. Believe me
I do. Way, way too much.

She asked me to teach a class on conflict and resolution.

No – I said, I like my little wars.

On the Suicide of My Cousin

Reservation. The restaurant wouldn't take us. I took you to an ice-cream shop. Your cone fell on the ground. I picked it up. Gave it to you. You said you tasted stone. We drove home. A week later, you'd drowned. We need an ombudsman. A home. To drive to. I talked to the man who reached for you. He said you suddenly got still. Your hand was a cloud.

The Arboretum

*8/27/90: I feel ashamed that I feel so sorry for myself – I am actually afraid
that I will have to life like this for years & that would be hell – but what can
I do to make myself happy? I guess I'll have to work at it. - James Kerr*

That day at the Arb—pink blanket, a bottle
of Coke, your cigarettes—we climbed the grassy hill,
vista of hemlock and maple, turquoise sky.

I sat crossed legged on the edge of shade
while you lay back on your elbows in the sun
smoking a joint, your eyes locked in smiles.

We flew through that day, admired the Frisbee-catching
dogs and the reverent quiet. We didn't know
that language of AZT or Elivil, we weren't yet talking

in vowels, still able to hold to consonants.
Later you would conjure up that day, hang on to it
like a piece of sodden wood not yet ready to do down.

To Amélie,

we can end in a mirage, but I'm hoping for seasons of
piracy where we—together—board the ships of the
colonizers and light sails on fire with a love like a
string of mountains set on fire, a museum-fire where
all of the bodies of false history burn

Refusing to Ride *The Creator*

My cousin wears a red bandanna, green tank top,
can't wait for the line to wing its way

to the metal pew she'll climb into
                              with faith. I refuse

to trust a track tended by a tattered man
who may be drunk.

I watch her ride her little kayak into the sky—

imagine the view from up there & fear
the fall.

I'm not brave. Not about this.

I've hitch-hiked through canyons
gone off in cars rippling with danger
— been thrown around

by love, & its escape. Look how convinced she is
            that no matter how jostled
there is cotton candy in the end.

Standing in Line at the V.A.

we have to put our hands against a red line on the
wall, a voice barking at my knees, we cannot take our
hands off the red tape on the wall, this is Chicago, a
city made of peonies, I meant a wall of pennies, I
mean a penny-city, the one that MLK said was the
most racist in the world, even more so than the south
with its dollar-cities, with its slave-metropoles, its
dancers starving for ones, its fluttering leaves of pain,
and the man in front of me has no legs, his legs are
storied somewhere, the prose-burial I cannot write

Childless

When I am old
no one

will ask me
why

I am crying.

Strangers will think
it is for...

when really
what I might want

is a cool,
sweet
slice
of watermelon.

No one
will ask me

what I want.

Ron Riekki

3 Lines for My Father

his childhood was a werewolf, but he still emerged as a church, a good church, the kind where the words are real and the candles have true flames, where the window isn't stained; it's open to God

Another Spring

Spring sounds of territory from a chickadee
     it's mine, it's mine

and so much work proving
               that it is.

Have you noticed the hawks?
They know
where the nests are.

The heart grows talons
holds to what it wants
works to claim its domain,
to imagine touch
that will sustain.

Everything has burst into bloom.

The irises are chatty tongues.
The tulips – thick stems in gold crowns.

It's spring.

A terror trapezes in me.

Ron Riekki

Eating Chili with My Girlfriend

we're too tired to fight, thank God, the day has taken
our bones, our horses, so we lie down in chairs with
bowls on our guts and spoon warmth that makes her
laugh as loud as falling off low ladders

After
   for Linda

I sat on the porch swing listening to the bees
praying in the lilacs. I thought of that scar

carved into her forehead. She told me
a box fell from a shelf in the garage.

I tried to remember what she said the day before.
She said, *he is sick.* She said, *leaving,* and

lawyers. She said, *unlucky,* and something
about not telling her mother. She never

said that she was scared.
She never said, *restraining order.*

If only I had had the chance I would have
given him the old *if you ever... again.* We

would have told everyone about him, built
a fortress with that knowledge.

I sat on the porch swing listening to the gospel of bees,
surveyed her life, then changed the ending.

Ron Riekki

I'll Vote for Anything that Moves

I'll vote for a tattoo.
I'll vote for a goose if it was able to look straight into a camera.
I'll vote for a newspaper as long as it's half correct.
I'll vote for a dock.
I'll vote for an ocean, if there's not too much garbage in it,
and I can stand a helluva lot of garbage.
I'll vote for a song.
I'll vote for a cobra. I actually kind of like cobras. I don't know why.
They keep killing me.
I keep waking up in coffins.
The lever in front of me.
I yank it like it actually holds secrets.

Capture Theory

A fly flew in with the swing of the door,
batted itself against the window.
            What were my choices?

Who can con a creature with compound eyes?

I could let it fly & land, fly
until it wore itself out.

I'm sorry played in my head as though

the world's traps were my project to undo.
Maybe not the world's, but this one, & others.

My mother once wrote: *You kids are wonderful
despite me.* What kind of a trap is that?

I can't explain why I threw that letter
out. Can't explain survival, or why

I lured that fly to the door by closing
the blinds; let darkness seize the house.

I knew it would find a way to save itself,
knew it would find the light.

My Girlfriend Wants Kid, Not Marriage (Part I)

She wants addiction, not beer.
She says the house should not have a roof
that roofs are overrated.
I show her a picture of God.
She asks me why She'd pose like that.

I tell her it was a roller coaster;
She was scared as hell.
The wolves come to the door.
I let them in. They go straight
for the good China.

They ignore the bad Switzerland.
There is a long history of suicide in my family.
There is a short amount of mathematics involved
in counting the dead. We just consider them
as one. A student in class says.

Luna Moth

Rarely seen. Lives only five-eight days.

A cabin porch, one light, everything still
as West Virginia granite —

the trees close-in around us like spires,
and memory. A train's distant coda
hums, sanctify, sanctify, sanctify,

when an moth, wings the size of a man's hand,
urgent and delicate as a first kiss, shows up
like an answer.

How can anything as short-lived as this
be so luminous?

I want you to think what I think,

see it as amazing   all that work to get here
attach it to something we both want.

I want us to be full of mouth and wings.

Say something. Say, *bodacious*, say, *cocoon*, say,
chance, say, *want* and *have.* Say, *us.*

Say, *there must be a god.*

My Girlfriend Wants Kid, Not Marriage (Part II)

"I don't mind natural disasters.
There are too many people in the world."
Another student says, "Where I live,
they keep all the windows open
in the skyscrapers, hoping people

will jump out. I notice the open window.
I tell them it's the first floor.
A student doesn't care, leaps out.
He tumbles into the picker bushes.
I hear his screams even now, as we sleep.

A Lesson About Boys

As a kid I learned science from my brother
who turned the sun on innocent ants
and fried them with a magnifying glass.

I liked the effect—sun as source, glass as catalyst—
but I could never bring myself to vaporize
a living creature because it's so cool.

Later, he got into trouble at school
for smacking a kid on the back of the head
as he leaned over the drinking fountain,

the kid's teeth connecting with metal.
There was an issue of blood
and angry parents.

When he turned his fist toward me
I grabbed his wrist. Before we hit the ground
my brother's hands

became a system of knowledge, general truths
about boys: I learned to walk around them slowly,
be especially careful on sunny days.

Tina Turner

I fell in love with her
as a youth.
I tell this to my girlfriend
when we're in France,
visiting her father.
They get in an argument.
At the end, she shouts out,
"Oh, Papa!"

and it reminds me of a tuba,
the rhythm of the words.
I think of oom-pah-pah,
the car that crashes
into the parade,
killing seven drummers.
It all makes me think
of the life of Tina Turner.

Bad Dog

Mom was still in her robe when the bell rang.
I was five. It was summer. There was a cop at the door.

I stood next to my mother on the front porch
as the officer explained why he was writing

yet another ticket: Blackie had gotten out again.
A lady complained that he molested her French Poodle,

and can't we do something about that dog.
No sir, thank you sir, sorry sir,

and the cop left. Mom turned to open the front door.

We were locked out. She rang the bell.
I remember my father yelling from inside,

someone's at the door, answer the god-damned door.
Mom rang the bell, and rang that bell.

She said, shit. She pulled her robe in closer,
angry at dad, angry at Blackie,

and I felt her anger fall all over me.
I knew that I could easily climb through the milk chute.

I knew, even then, that I would have to save her.

Rikkaruohoja

Noin noukit rikkaruohoja,
oi äiti, taimitarhastas
ja kohta kaikk' on puhdasta
sun pienoisessa puistossas.

Mut kohta sydän lapseskin
jo versoo rikkaruohoja -
kun sielläi, äiti armahin,
sa saisit yhtä puhdasta!

by Eino Leino (1878-1926)

Weeds

Like picked weeds, there,
oh mother, your nursery of grey hairs
and here is the point: all is purest—
even the sun is a miniature forest.

But soon the heart is skin,
already weeds sprouting—
there! poor mother;
you are just as pure.

translated by Ron Riekki

The Cynic

Doesn't understand
the word
sweet.

It seems to be
a word that drifts
between   *mother* & *donuts.*

When she,
the cynic,
hears that a man
wants a woman
who is   *sweet*

what she hears is
I want a woman
who employs
silence,
is not too
ambitious,

makes good desserts.

**The Wealthy are Those Who Have Jobs and They Look at Me
Like I am a Rope**

that I can use to hang myself.
Standing in the unemployment line,
you can feel the rage for jobs.
I met a woman there, jobless too,
who took me to a diner and we ate

scrambled eggs and she asked me
if I wanted children and I could tell
if I answered wrong, that I would
never hear from her again and I said
yes and she said, "You're unemployed"

and she said, "And I'm unemployed"
and she said, "The only thing we can
have is this" and she looked down
at the egg, unfinished, on her plate,
and you could see its future, its past.

Without

I'm lying in the back seat
  without a man
    to kiss,
just listening
to robins, some sparrows,
  a cardinal chipping an evening sermon.
The garden of lake
  breathes in the fading day – as blue
    as unwrapped iris.
I am here
 contemplating
  the way sunlight bleeds
through the maple leaves,
and the way I left
  because trees
could not interest you.
And because you did not know
  the sweetness of tapped sugar.

Ron Riekki

Sonnet 22:
To the Veterans Who Continue to Live Despite the Intrusions

At the V.A. office, the person who checks you in
looks like she hates veterans more than she hates
life itself. You wonder about the broken spines,
the way the moon looks suicidal today, the sun
battling for the sky. I have had three counselors,
one was Satan, the other was a simulacra of
the resurrection, but the one I have now is human,
makes me think I'll survive winter. Twenty-two
vets a day kill themselves. In Diego, my bunk-
mate would chase chickens, telling me that if he
caught one, he'd choke it. We'd stare out at the
search-and-rescue boats and the sun would be
hellishly beautiful, death's ass on the horizon,
only the ability to escape, to wait, to cling to air.

Joy Gaines-Friedler

Huntress

A sponge ball in her mouth. She struts.
A mouth full of surety. The boys
shuck her off. Her mood swings like an addict.

My father's plan is to stay alive, beat cancer
the way he beat anti-Semitic managers at the car
companies in the forties, shook-off

poverty selling used pieces of soap
door to door. It was a time when strangers
weren't something to fear, when fortitude

and self-reliance sent all those boys
to sign-up for war, willingly, wave goodbye
to their *gals* from street cars, never speak

of what they saw there. My father, in a cottage
on Walled Lake, exiled during The Depression.
No tumor will rob him of what he knows himself to be.

I can beat this thing, he tells me. *I know I can.*

The Huntress has just found another sponge ball,
struts out of the room, a world full of triumph in her mouth.

I Ask the Class
Who Else Has Been in the Military
and the Class is Silent

not can-we-have-a-moment-of-silence
silence, not we're-looking-at-a-row-of-
Arlington-tombstones silence, but rather
a who-the-hell-cares silence where rain
falls outside and you can hear it jogging
down the side of the building like it has
a big date tonight and wants to turn into
a supermodel in super-seconds and I say
in the most academic language that I can
possibly muster, "oh, forget it" like war
can be wiped out by quitting speaking.

Black Ice

The night has become a car slipping silently
Into a ditch after touching another
Then recoiling from such intimacy.

What falls does not fall
But rather thickens,
        but we knew this
When we left the house –
The day so vulnerable.

Night has become a police car
Herding drivers off the freeway.

Like a cataract, sleet claims the windshield.

Make it home – everyone's cold mantra.
One more mile.
One more time.

Make it home – Along a known
Yet, unexpected hazard.

We are saying nothing.
We are cleated.
We are knuckling through.

Ron Riekki

I Am Eaten by the Dust and Born to Sleep

My narcolepsy turns me into a closed hard-
ware store, the shelves empty for the day,

my sex cataplexy deep so that I feel choked
by touch, alone in the day, my easy bones

turned to shackles, the feel of an inability
to rake out breath, and the doctor says

it will only get worse, that there is no
care for funding, that it's not a sexy dis-

ease, and so I put out a No Parking sign
and drift away, unable to drive, the cabin

in the horror movie before anyone arrives
other than the days' permanent sick ghosts.

The Pool

Light floats in the maples above the pool.
A pair of mallards we've named
Carl & Anita crash-land in the shallow end.

They do us no harm.
We let them swim.

We suppose a kind of faith—

when the sun spills through the trees
and spotlights a small spider on the coping.

This morning, before first light,
an owl called from the distance.

I went out to the pool, spooked a feral cat,
then sat in the dark to listen. The trees

swayed in silence.

We've lived through the dying. And
there will be more. For now

 Carl is happy
to follow Anita to the deep end.
They move easily together.

They are not going anywhere.

Here

our love—

a river
in a fireplace.

Florida Clouds

White lies of palm trees, teethy
alligators, the face of lost fathers,
and states... the mitten of Michigan.

Weighty vessels of vapor
here's to your emptiness. Ethereal
as anger, which is more about
loneliness than anything tangible
 – more like air
than mass. Crazy
how you spread yourself thin,
then disappear.

It would be foolish
to think of memory as something solid
or tried to hold on to its misty edges,
or tried to live inside it.

I know deception, you billowing clouds of Florida—
(sometimes bellowing wind makers).

May your rage explode,
then huff into silence.

Trochaic (Art)
for Bill Berkson

Life is painful,
Racing but a drag.

Cars are made by Detroit,
That's a partial lie.

"What's wrong with this book,"
A Detroit poet says,

"There's too much traffic—and
Too many traffic lovers!"

"You a taxi driver?"
"Nah, I just write poems."

Test Trials

What if the word *deficiency* had no need to coexist
with *auto* and *immune.* Or, you had been born five years later.
What if the cocktail caught up to you. Maybe

we would be mocking The Emmys, choosing color swatches
for wall paint, laughing about the time a bee flew into your car,
we nearly lost our minds, finally one of us (was it you?) opened the
door. We looked at each other and laughed a full five minutes.

There are 745,000 results for AIDS CURE in a Google search
– and not one of them is.

Now I'm looking at the blinking cursor, feel the words *curse* and *cure*
in those perfectly straight vertical heartbeats – right here
you would give yourself away and say, *never straight, only forward.*

*"A flatline is an electrical time sequence measurement that shows no
activity."*

I wonder how God measures time.

They say there are parallel universes
where the thinking of a Thing makes it so. What if I think you
smoking a Tareyton, a cup of coffee, notice
 that slight tremor in your hand.
Now I'm thinking: you never met that man,
didn't make that date, had a flat tire, changed your mind.

My Roommate, the Cop Tells Me He's Moving Out Soon

He says this in front of the blinds
that won't close. He says he's moving in
with a nurse, that cops all marry nurses,
that I should become a nurse so that I could
marry a cop and I want to tell him
that I hope I never get married and definitely
not to a cop and it's silent a bit and then he tells me
about a kid who got shot in the eye last night
and the bullet ricocheted around in his head
and came out the other eye, getting stuck in the socket,
and he looks at me waiting for the question I'd ask
but I wanted to ask him if he can move out today
or not at all because I need money for the rent
but instead I just said, "How old was the kid?"
and he said, "I don't know, thirty" and he pulled
the blind and it fell on the floor so that the sun
basically beat the shit out of the apartment.

Monarch Metamorphosis

We watch them grow stocky
in their striped summer shirts,

their blind-eye canes of antennae.
Spiders & fire ants gorge on them.
Mornings I take my coffee outside,
examine each leaf. Search.

Seek their preservation.
My friend was killed—
there is no other way to say it—

by the man who once sat with her
in the shade of the chalk maple. Gone
overnight. Drought sensitive, my search

is the single inseparable constant of my life.
I keep hoping for a chrysalis
push myself toward the next stage. Anxious

about the caterpillars' survival
When I was ten I believed that no one
noticed the trees but me. I'd never seen milkweed.

Never seen a gun.
How do any of us survive?

The Doctor Tells Me Not to Worry about My Thyroid

because I can't afford to do anything about it anyway.
The books in the V.A. waiting room have been stolen
for drug money. I walk out to my car and it looks like
it has been smoking a pack-a-day for eighteen years,
the door coughing when I open it, and I drive deep

into Los Angeles, its nicotine everything, and at home
my apartment looks like it's coming apart, as if its name
meant to explain it all, and I'm coming apart but in a good
way, where your past gets left in the dust, and the dust
feels like what you see after a motorcycle has ripped by.

Foreclosed

My parents things have gone to die
on my brother's wall, shoved together
in his apartment like a hoard of herded
merchandise, stolen by a compulsive thief.

When one has earned nothing
one craves everything.

Are we trained to be crow-like?
Are lacquered dressers that don't fit the walls,
& crystal glassware that will never be used,
the shiny crow objects we covet?

He hoards, to fill the empty.

Trauma gets remembered in your bones.

Come May, the smell of gun powder
permeates the air.

Come August, I become a mother
I've never been. Bleeding again.

Come September, I hold the hand of my
best friend, tell him to *let go*.

What happens when the birds are gone, is this:

The birds are gone.

Ron Riekki

I Keep Getting into Fistfights with God Every Sunday

I need to just give up and sit in the back pew
like a child in the good old days when I'd sleep
through church. Now I fight with politics
and movie ticket prices and youtube ads, as if
my church is wrath, the wrinkles in my lungs
foreshadowing a hundred thunderbolts landing
on my failures. But I argue back that I believe
in God, otherwise I wouldn't fight Him. It takes
faith to argue, the belief in belief, how moronic
we all are, and the monk tells me that not
thinking is better than being naked in July.

Hitting The Deer

I will have to forgive
the weight of her

like a tree limb lobbed
against the windshield,

have to forgive her
eyes black, wild

as a stampede, the
explosion of the radiator,

fur, hide
sliced into the grill.

I will have to forgive
her lying in the road

ruined, & the sound
of the cop's gun

discharging a bullet
into her head.

I will have to forgive the fawn
she may have left folded in the woods,

& myself wrung,
rung in boom & echo.

My Three Days Working as a Clown

I couldn't handle the fear. I thought it might be laughs,
but there is sheer terror in minimum wage. The children

would scream as if they were attempting to heat their throats
with noise. I'd take off my nose and hair and that seemed

to make them feel like a skeleton was taking off its bones
right in front of them, the horror of subtraction. If I spoke,

it was worse, my noise shaky and awkward, so that I just
remained silent and frightened myself, their assassination

stares, my time-clock waiting, their clutching at hips,
my desperation for rent, something hilarious in it all.

Whom I Dare Not Read

Sometimes it is best not to read
                              another poet
        forgive me
but the railroad tracks—
    what one might call the *great subdivide*
                              (I just made that up)
feels like something stolen from me.

Like that cool book by Malcolm X
that went missing from my bookcase
after a visit from my nephew.

Should I be ashamed of this? I'm not.

Of course, this has nothing to do with
the book or the tracks – which are merely
innocent until the horrifying power of
the engine pulls with it all that (I mean, *my*) cargo

or the faces of westbound seekers – some,
I bet one for sure, is scribbling that perfect line—
the line I
        already wrote—
almost.

The Mountain Lion Walks by My Guard Gate

Wind. The cheap boom barrier had been shaking all night,
shook by ghosts, the biohazard-packed building behind it
steady as Hell. I was fighting falling asleep, punching

nightmares to death, an epistaxis of night terrors with eyes
wide nothing.
Then five deer running with hemotympanum
fear; the moment their hooves hit the asphalt, they skidded,

falling to their thin knees, bouncing back up again, and diving
into the anorexic bushes that surround our everything here.
Then peace.   Then a shadow the color of murder. I slid

my kiosk door shut, soft, taking my eyes off the thing
that was no longer a thing, just a thin memory.
I found out
the next day, the tail end of a graveyard shift, the cars

arriving like thyroid storms, that they deliver subpoenas
to your workplaces, for the extra embarrassment, publicity,
the annulment, the dissolution, how life's split into vivisections.

Joy Gaines-Friedler

Domestic Violence

The mauve couch in the family room
where she sat folding laundry

watching television with her mother.
The door he entered with the key

he had not yet relinquished.
The argument no one will recall.

The gun he bought that day at K-Mart.
The hole through the couch she barely

escaped. The second in the door frame
of the kitchen where she reached the phone,

911 on speed dial. Her mother's hands
that grabbed his arm. The way he shook them off.

The explosion that cracked through the ceiling
and spit bits of plaster and yellow paint.

The fourth blast that scored a bullet seared gouge
across the innocent linoleum, shattering floor molding.

The kitchen table she tried to wear as a shield.
The sour smell of gunpowder.

Two more holes
from the rounds none of us will escape.

Ron Riekki

My Vietnamese Girlfriend

tells me she could not afford to go to high school,
that she went to work cleaning out the wax
from people's ears. She looks into my ears
and tells me they are good, that I know how
to clean myself, and then she plucks a hair
from my cheek, as she scans my body, her eyes
devastating me, the electrical power lines of her mouth,
and I take her finger and slide an invisible ring
onto it, telling her that we are married now,
invisible married, and there is an invisible orchestra
playing the most beautiful invisible song
as a thousand invisible people applaud
at how much I long for her, and she sits on top
of me and says that she prefers the visible world
with its cerumen and poverty, its lips
and embarrassment, and she bites the New Orleans
of my lip while staring into me, prayers of wanting.

Tucson

8/6/89: "Right now I just want to stay healthy and, well, alive."
9/29/89:"They should have deals at the hospital - every 4th transfusion FREE!"
--James Kerr

In Tucson the cacti and I sat
vigil while you slept.

I watched them turn gold
in the waning sun;

admired their strong arms,
and wondered which pull

was more powerful,
the sun or gravity.

The moon arrived before
the sky refused to give up its blue -

your favorite color. I waited for you
to return from this disease that

kept interfering with the sunset
and stole your energy.

How long did I sleep? you asked.
It doesn't matter, I said.

Inside we opened a can of soup.

I Knew a Guy Who Kept Getting Robbed

They robbed him in a bathroom
twice.
They robbed him of his laptop.

They robbed him of his phone
so he couldn't even call the police.
They robbed him of his hair.

They robbed him of snow.
They robbed him of his coma.
They robbed his parents' parents' parents.

In the bathroom, he said the worst thing
wasn't losing the money,
but was the taste of the wall, the bitterness of Trump.

The woman receptionist for my PTSD counselor
at the V.A. said to me,
"Why don't you just get over it?"

Come Over, Bring Keats

He who saddens/At the thought of idleness cannot be idle
                                                                            - John Keats

Bring your booster rocket.
Burn through what's left of this catastrophe.
Leave your dusty boots by the bed - plant a flag on "us."

Years later you will say
"I know now what you wanted."

Yourself—your soul—in pity give me all...

There will be no comfort in that. Only
reflections, like gazing at iridescent glazes
through museum glass. Artifacts
whose histories cling

the way I lifted the felt-lined bottom of a jewelry box
found a tiny tintype of you there,
your strong face trapped in shadow.
A small hole in the metal – makes it a charm.

Was it a vision, or a waking dream?
        Fled is that music:—Do I wake or sleep?

Flat & smooth against my fingers, I held it.
I hold it.

A kind of radiant heat still burning.

The Jesus Painting at My Grandma's

used to scare the hell out of me,
the eyes like a quarterback,
and even the colors of the sky
behind Him seemed like they'd over-

dosed on ecstasy, and when I asked
my grandma why she had a cover
of Fangoria on her wall, she said,
"Everyone hears everything everyone thinks."

Last Trip To The Barber

My father heron-frail
craned his neck into the wrinkled sky
                              as I drove—

said, *Sometimes I see the face of my father in the clouds.*

This must have been a trick—
the way what once stung your skin—
up close, is something delicate with wings
& its own compound body.

I too looked up, seeking
a face or symbol, something of angels or
the terrifying.

A comfortable silence fell between us.

Where did this trust come from?
& that look from the guys at the barber shop
when they first saw him—

their eyes like startled cats
turned swiftly to contentment.

Your dad is an amazing guy.

What we didn't know, couldn't know,
might fill the sky.

The Gun Owner/Drunk

A
guy
who lived
right next door
said he tried to shoot
a cloud to see if it would bleed.
When the fog started rolling in, we felt drowned in sky
like blood was owning the earth.
The reality is that bullets have to land somewhere.

Communion

3/28/90: I'm injecting Interferon in my stomach, taking pills, DDI—
Jesus what an array. - James Kerr

Our last conversation you said,
that all your life   you'd been *a shadow.*

Then you said, *it is time for this to end*

and shocked me with   *pray for me.*

I thought of our ritual of passing around the bong
Sunday mornings, how you called it *Morning Mass,*

& the Communion I took while attending church with you one Sunday
    surprised by the way the wafer melted in my mouth

before I returned to kneel next to your laughing shoulders,
    your eyes a bit scared for my brazen Jewish soul.

Before you slipped away from me I wanted to remind you

how fun it was to slide Kahlua into our coffee,
dance to Stairway to Heaven, stay up all night

talking about God & fathers —despite the lesions
& new words like *lesions & pneumatoid*— I'm thinking,

maybe I will lie and say that
I held the hand of my best friend as he died from AIDS,

which I do—only, it isn't a lie.

War Poetry

I don't read war poetry
because I was in a war.
I can't imagine reading war poetry
after you've been in a war.
I write war poetry sometimes
because I was in a war
so I don't have to do any research.
I just think back to the helicopter on fire
and then I write a line like
The helicopter was on fire
and then in class they tell me
that I have to describe the fire
and I start to do it,
saying what bodies look like melting
and then they tell me to stop
and so I stop.

Magazines that Joy's poems in this volume appeared in. . .

Accents
A&U Magazine
Bear River Review
Big Scream
Black Fork Review
Broadkill River Review
Cholla Needles
Controlled Burn
Cumberland Review
Driftwood
Hazmat Review
Litchfield Review
Michigan Poets
Montucky Review
Not By Might
One Art
Panopoly
Peninsula Poets
Poetry in Performance
San Pedro River Review
Silver Boomers
Swallow The Moon
The Michigan Poet
Third Wednesday

Anthologies
Bloomsbury Anthology of Contemporary Jewish American Poetry
The Path To Kindness, by James Crews, 2021
Composing Poetry, by Gerry LaFemina, 2017

Magazines that Ron's poems in this volume appeared in. . .

*82 Review
Barking Sycamores
Blast Furnace
B O D Y
Border Crossing
Buck Off Magazine
Crack the Spine
Cruel Garters
decomP
elsewhere
FIVE:2:ONE
Gambling the Aisle
Gloom Cupboard
Great Lakes Review
Invisible City
Juked
Leaping Clear
Muse-Pie Press Shot Glass Journal
Muse-Pie Press The Fib Review
OVS Magazine
Rattle
The Main Street Rag
The Monarch Review
The Rupture
The Swamp Literary Magazine
The Whorticulturalist
Tipton Poetry Journal
Toe Good
Torrid Literature Journal
Wilderness House Literary Review
Your Impossible Voice

Joy Gaines-Friedler

For 20 years Joy Gaines-Friedler made her living as a photographer. She is the author of 5 books of poetry, including *Capture Theory,* a Forward Review Indie Press Book of The Year, Finalist. Joy teaches Memoir & Poetry for non-profits & communities at risk in S.E. Michigan.

author photo by Amelie Jumel

Ron Riekki

Ron Riekki's books include *Posttraumatic*, and
My Ancestors are Reindeer Herders and I Am Melting in Extinction.

Made in the USA
Middletown, DE
02 July 2023

34454066R00064